SOUTH AFRICA

Written by Esta Saint-Claire

COUNTRIES of the WORLD

PowerKiDS press

Published in 2025
by The Rosen Publishing Group, Inc.
2544 Clinton Street, Buffalo, NY 14224

Written by: Esta Saint-Claire
Edited by: Elise Carraway
Designed by: Miranda Tremere

Cataloging-in-Publication Data

Names: Saint-Claire, Esta.
Title: South Africa / Esta Saint-Claire.
Description: Buffalo, NY : PowerKids Press, 2025. | Series: Countries of the world | Includes glossary and index.
Identifiers: ISBN 9781499447248 (pbk.) | ISBN 9781499447255 (library bound) | ISBN 9781499447262 (ebook)
Subjects: LCSH: South Africa--Juvenile literature.
Classification: LCC DT1719.S256 2025 | DDC 968--dc23

Manufactured in the United States of America
CPSIA Compliance Information: Batch #CSPK25. For further information contact Rosen Publishing at 1-800-237-9932.

Image Credits
All images are courtesy of Shutterstock.com, unless otherwise specified. With thanks to Getty Images, Thinkstock Photo and iStockphoto. Cover – Arnold.Petersen, Richard Cavalleri, InnaFelker, Anna Kosheleva, GoodStudio. 2 – PACO COMO. 4–5 – Andrew Minsk, kavram. 6–7 – Ryan Lansdown, Salt Rock Digital. 8–9 – Sunshine Seeds, greenaperture, Sakura Image Inc, Pixel-Shot. 10–11 – pixelheadphoto digitalskillet, koldo_studio. 12–13 – Sunshine Seeds. 14–15 – Heinrich van Tonder, Lucia.Pinto, Julie Scheveneels. 16–17 – DiversityStudio, The White House from Washington, DC, Public domain via Wikimedia Commons. 18–19 – Monkey Business Images, Paolo Bona. 20–21 – Morne van Jaarsveld, Rowan Patrick Photos. 22–23 – g_tech, Passakorn Umpornmaha, Eric Isselee, mariakray, michaeljung.

CONTENTS

Words that look like this can be found in the glossary on page 24.

WHERE IS SOUTH AFRICA?

South Africa is located in the southernmost part of the African continent.

There are around 60 million people living in South Africa. There are three capital cities of South Africa: Pretoria, Bloemfontein, and Cape Town.

LANDSCAPE AND WEATHER

Most of South Africa has a moderate climate, which means it is neither too hot nor too cold. However, in the mountains, winters can be very cold.

On the east coast of South Africa, the weather is almost tropical.

RELIGION

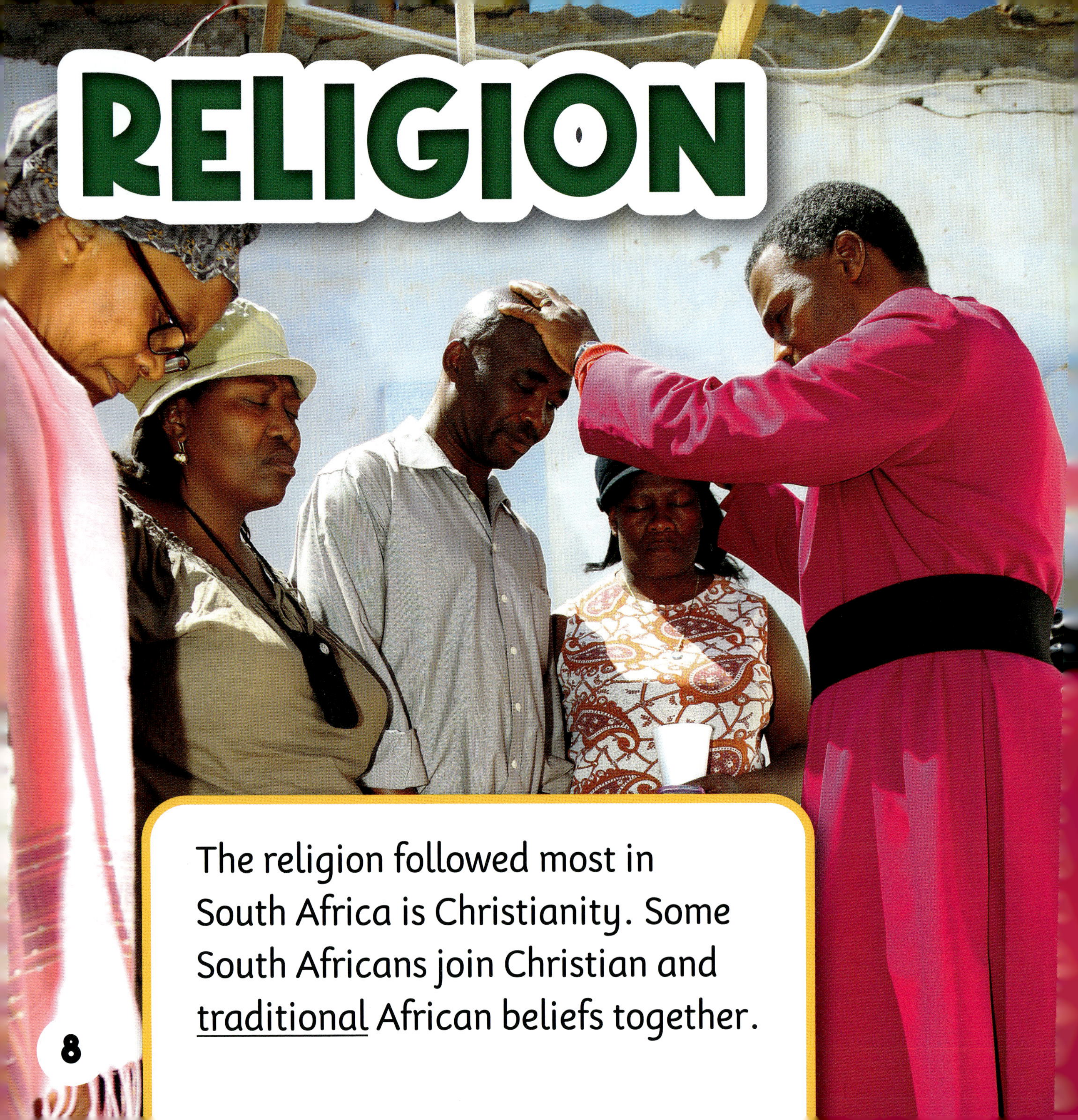

The religion followed most in South Africa is Christianity. Some South Africans join Christian and traditional African beliefs together.

Other religions followed are Hinduism, Islam, and Judaism.

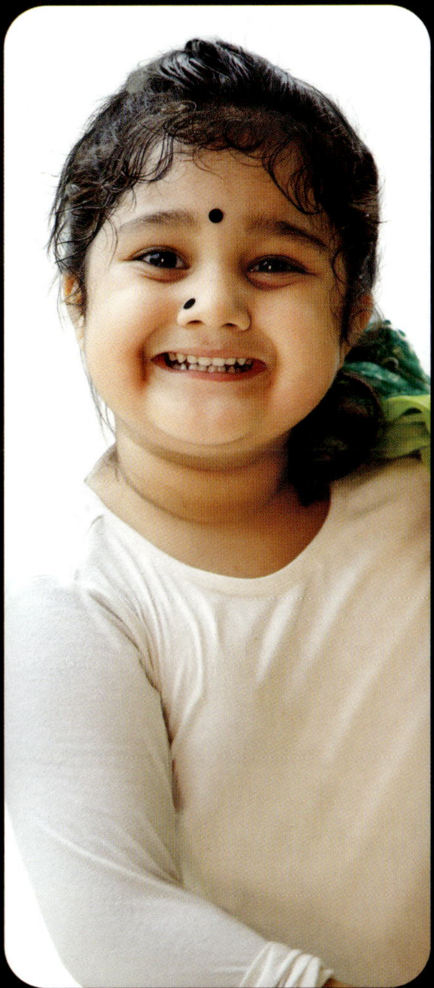

Hindu child

Muslim child

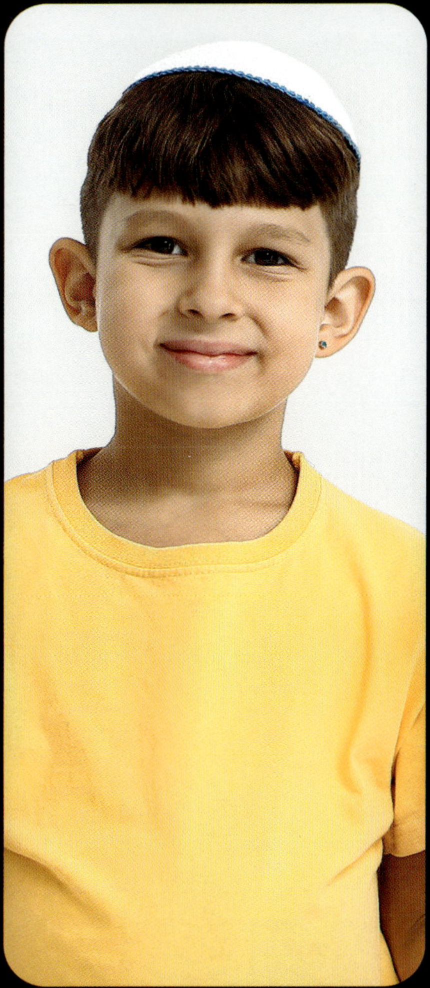

Jewish child

FAMILIES

Family life is different all over South Africa. Children who live in the countryside usually live with their siblings, parents, and grandparents. They sometimes live with their aunts, uncles, and cousins too.

Children who live in cities usually only live with their siblings and parents.

SCHOOL

Children in South Africa are usually six or seven years old when they start primary school. For the first few years, children learn their own language. Later, they study a second and sometimes even a third language too.

Primary school usually starts at 7:30 AM and finishes at 1:00 PM or later.

HOME

People in South Africa who live in cities often live in apartments. Wealthy families may live outside of the cities in large houses.

In some places, round buildings with thatched roofs can be seen. These buildings, called rondavels, are not normally used as homes today. They are based on the traditional buildings of the Xhosa people of South Africa.

CLOTHING

Traditionally, people in South Africa wear brightly colored clothing that is suited to the climate of the area they live in.

In the cities, many people wear modern clothing.

Nelson Mandela wearing a Madiba shirt

Nelson Mandela, a former South African president, often wore Madiba shirts, which are made from batik silk. They are named after his family name, which is also "Madiba."

SPORTS

When the weather is warm in South Africa, many families like to go to the beach and swim. Soccer is a popular sport played in South Africa.

Rugby is also a very popular sport in South Africa. Their national team won the World Cup in 1995, 2007, 2019, and 2023.

FOOD

The people of South Africa come from many backgrounds, which shows in their cuisine. Spicy sausages, called boerewors, are cooked on a special grill called a braai.

A braai is a bit like a barbecue.

Biltong is a dried meat that is popular in South Africa. It is now sold all over the world.

FUN FACTS

South Africa is home to many wild animals, such as lions, giraffes, and hippopotamuses.

South Africa has 11 official languages, including Zulu, Afrikaans, Xhosa, and English.

Drivers drive on the left-hand side of the road in South Africa.

The first human heart transplant was performed in a Cape Town hospital in 1967.

GLOSSARY

batik a method of dyeing fabrics using wax

climate the weather in a large area

cuisine food that is usually found in a certain country

modern to do with recent or present times

national to do with things that are shared by or important to people in a country

siblings brothers and sisters

traditional to do with beliefs, customs, or ways of behaving that have been around for a long time

transplant an operation to move a body part from one place to another

tropical very warm and wet

INDEX